NATIONAL GEOGRAPHIC OUR WORLD

Tortoise and Hare's Race

Based on an Aesop's Fable

by Zoe McLoughlin

NATIONAL GEOGRAPHIC LEARNING

CENGAGE Learning

One afternoon in the park, Hare sees Tortoise. Tortoise is exercising.

"Why are you doing that?" says Hare. "I don't like to exercise. It makes me tired."

"Exercise makes my muscles and bones strong," says Tortoise. "I get plenty of exercise! And I don't eat junk food."

"I like junk food!" Hare says. "I eat lots of it."

3

"I don't have to be in shape," says Hare.
"I can win a race against you any day!"

"Really?" says Tortoise. "I don't think you can.
Let's race next weekend."

All week Tortoise exercises to get ready for the race.

Hare just sleeps and eats lots of junk food.

"I'm fast already," says Hare. "I can beat Tortoise any day!"

On the day of the race, Tortoise feels ready. "I'm so fast," says Hare. "This is going to be easy." Bear blows a whistle, and the race starts!

Hare is fast! At first, he runs far in front of Tortoise. He runs so far that Tortoise can't see him anymore.

Tortoise says, "Hare is fast, but I'm in good shape. I can catch up."

"I am far ahead of Tortoise, but this is hard,"
says Hare. "I need something to drink!"
Hare stops for a drink and a rest.

Hare falls asleep, but Tortoise keeps running.
Soon Tortoise runs past Hare.
"Hare looks tired," says Tortoise. "I guess he
doesn't get enough sleep."

Finally, Hare wakes up. He sees Tortoise is far ahead of him!

"Ahh!" says Hare. "Tortoise is far ahead. I have to catch up!"

Now Hare has to run FAST!

FINISH

Hare runs fast, but he can't catch up with Tortoise.
Tortoise wins the race!

"Can I exercise with you tomorrow?"
asks Hare.

"Sure!" says Tortoise. "I can help you get
in shape. But no more junk food!"

Facts About Sleep

All living things need sleep to stay healthy. But not all living things need the same amount of sleep.

Experts say that humans of different ages need different amounts of sleep.

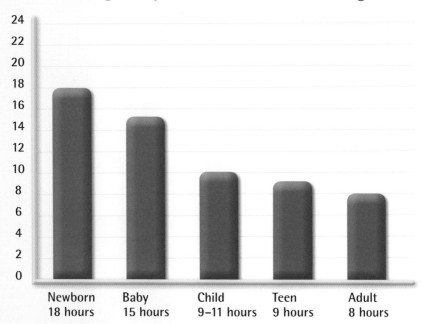

Average Sleep Humans Need at Different Ages

| Newborn 18 hours | Baby 15 hours | Child 9–11 hours | Teen 9 hours | Adult 8 hours |

Newborn: 18 hours

Child: 9-11 hours

Adult: 8 hours

Different animals need different amounts of sleep, too.

For example, giraffes can go weeks without sleeping. They get no more than two hours of sleep a day. Brown bats get the most sleep. They sleep almost all day!

Brown Bat
20 hours

House Cat
12 hours

African Elephant
3 hours

Giraffe
2 hours

Fun with Good Health

Unscramble the word for each picture.

| bones | exercise | muscles | sleep |

sclumes

1. _muscles_

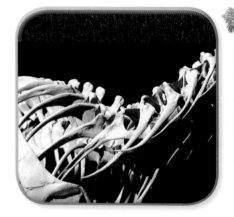

enobs

2. _____

plees

3. _____

eixcerse

4. _____

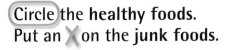

Circle the **healthy foods.**
Put an ✗ on the **junk foods.**

Write a list of three more healthy foods and three more junk foods. Use a bilingual dictionary if necessary.

Glossary

blows pushes air through the lips

hare an animal similar to a rabbit, but larger

hours amounts of time that are 60 minutes

race a contest to see who can run fastest

tortoise an animal with four legs and a hard shell that lives mostly on land

whistle something you blow into that makes a loud sound

wins be the first person to finish a race